BEST OF SHANGHAI
YOUR #1 ITINERARY PLANNER FOR WHAT TO SEE, DO, AND EAT

Wanderlust Pocket Guides

Planning a trip or looking for travel inspiration?
Check out our other Wanderlust Pocket Travel Guides on Amazon:

BEST OF CHINA: YOUR #1 ITINERARY PLANNER FOR WHAT TO SEE, DO, AND EAT

BEST OF BEIJING: YOUR #1 ITINERARY PLANNER FOR WHAT TO SEE, DO, AND EAT

BEST OF JAPAN: YOUR #1 ITINERARY PLANNER FOR WHAT TO SEE, DO, AND EAT

BEST OF TOKYO: YOUR #1 ITINERARY PLANNER FOR WHAT TO SEE, DO, AND EAT

BEST OF KYOTO: YOUR #1 ITINERARY PLANNER FOR WHAT TO SEE, DO, AND EAT

BEST OF ITALY: YOUR #1 ITINERARY PLANNER FOR WHAT TO SEE, DO, AND EAT

BEST OF FLORENCE AND TUSCANY: YOUR #1 ITINERARY PLANNER FOR WHAT TO SEE, DO, AND EAT

BEST OF VENICE: YOUR #1 ITINERARY PLANNER FOR WHAT TO SEE, DO, AND EAT

BEST OF ROME: YOUR #1 ITINERARY PLANNER FOR WHAT TO SEE, DO, AND EAT

TABLE OF CONTENTS

Best of Shanghai

HOW TO USE THIS GUIDE

Every part of China is unique, but if you only have a few days, Shanghai is a good bet since the metropolitan is representative of modern China, while the surrounding towns offer a glimpse into the ancient country.

With this Wanderlust Pocket Guide, you can follow our tailored 3-day itinerary in Shanghai, which includes a daytrip to Hangzhou, Suzhou, or one of the famous water towns that look like Venice in the east. Alternatively, you can customize your stay using our "top experiences in Shanghai" section, and the subsequent detailed introduction to all the top sights, and experiences in this region. There is enough for as many days as you can spare!

We also introduce you to each district of Shanghai, and tell you where you should stay, and what you should eat during your stay, because we want to make sure you enjoy every single minute of your journey. Following this guide, you'll be sure to have tried all of Shanghai's best and most authentic dishes, and stayed in an area that makes sense for your trip.

If you have more than a few days, consider venturing into other parts of China. You can take an overnight trip to Xi'an, Beijing, Guilin, or fly into Hong Kong. Check out Wanderlust Pocket Guide Best of China or Best of Beijing for more information.

At the end of the guide, we have included some more practical information on visiting China, including visa requirements; best time to visit, currency, and an extensive list of survival Chinese phrases. Don't forget to consult these, to make sure your trip goes as smoothly as possible!

INTRODUCTION

This sprawling metropolis is the largest and most prosperous city in China. Over 23 million people call Shanghai home, rich and poor. The Chinese have a saying, "Shanghai is heaven for the rich, hell for the poor." And indeed, the city is alternately a fantastic wonderland filled with every pleasure imaginable, and for most inhabitants of the city, a place where they flock to from all over China, and work hard for the hopes of one day realizing their prosperous dreams.

The city is relatively young by Chinese standards. It first rose to prominence and gained an international reputation during the Colonial Era at the turn of the 20th century, when many westerners came to the specially designated "concession" districts. They lent Shanghai an international flair, leaving behind one of the richest collections of Art Deco buildings in the world. You can still see attractive buildings in classic Parisian style, Tudor style, and 1930s buildings reminiscent of the Gilded Age in New York, all of which stand not too far from the historic shikumen houses, which blend Chinese styles with European aesthetics, and are unique to Shanghai.

After some lean years under the new People's Republic of China, Shanghai has once again recovered its cosmopolitan flair since the country opened up to the world. Today, it is as modern and dazzling as Hong Kong and Tokyo, and is the undisputed financial and commercial center of China. In 2010, it hosted the World Expo, receiving the greatest number of visitors in the event's history. Today, the city dubbed the Pearl of the Orient and Paris of the East may just be the most alluring locale in all of Asia.

Jiang Nan

The geographic area known as "Jiang Nan", refers to lands south of the lower reaches of the Yangtze River, and includes the cities of Shanghai, Suzhou, Hangzhou, as well as parts of Jiangsu, Anhui, Jiangxi, and Zhejiang Provinces. Because the region's soil is fertile and its weather mild, Jiang Nan developed relatively early in Chinese history, and became prosperous through rice, clothing, and other trading activities. Aside from its busy commercial history, the area has always been a top tourist destination popular for peaceful canals, picturesque streets, and tasteful gardens in its many water towns.

TOP EXPERIENCES IN SHANGHAI

1. **Stroll Along the Bund in Shanghai, Where the Old Meets the New**
    On one bank of the Huangpu River stand the magnificent and varied Art Deco buildings left during Shanghai's Colonial Era from the early 1900's, while on the other, ultramodern skyscrapers from the last few decades of China's rapid economic development soar into the clouds. At night, both old and new glitter with neon lights. A walk along this stretch of Shanghai's famous riverside, known as the Bund, is definitely a stunning experience that even those from the most metropolitan cities will be impressed, and unable to forget.

2. **Experience Nanjing Road, the Time Square of China**

The neon lights along Nanjing Road are quite possibly even brighter than the lights in Time Square. This famous shopping street has everything from the most prestigious brands in the world, to the most affordable street fashion, not to mention tons of electronics, books, and any kind of food you can imagine. It's crowded on the weekend, but that's part of the street's bustling charm!

3. Walk through the French Concession, and Look at Colonial Architecture

The area formerly allocated to the French during Shanghai's Colonial era is full of interesting architecture that blends European aesthetics with traditional Chinese styles. Among the beautiful houses is the former residence of Sun Yat-sen, who was the "Father of the Nation".

4. **Sample Soup Dumplings and Shanghainese Cuisine**
    Shanghainese cuisine is known for being rich and slightly
    sweet. The most famous dish is soup dumpling, which is a
    delicate bun filled with pork, crab meat, and a delicious
    thick broth that comes dripping out when you bite into it.
    It's a must-try along with other Shanghainese dishes.

5. **Visit the Renowned Traditional Chinese Garden, Yu
    Yuan**
    Yu Garden, from the 1500's, is a tranquil place
    thoughtfully laid out according to Chinese "feng shui". Its
    grounds are beautifully landscaped, and its rooms
    sparingly but tastefully decorated. Experience how the
    wealthy and educated lived in Shanghai five hundred years
    ago.

6. **Shop for Local Snacks and Souvenirs near Temple of
    the Town God at Night**
    The Temple of the Town God has always been popular
    with locals wanting to make a wish, but the area near the

temple lights up at night, with many fun shops and local snacks. So be sure to stop by on an empty stomach, and eat and shop your way through.

7. **Take a Day Trip to a Water Town near Shanghai, and Experience "Jiang Nan"**
   The region around Shanghai, known as "jiang nan" in Chinese, is famous for its water towns, and the tranquil culture that has become associated with them. Each small water town, with its network of canals and classical houses along the water, is like Venice in China.

8. **Go to Suzhou for the Most Famous Classical Chinese Gardens**
   As beautiful as Yu Garden is, China's most famous classical gardens are in Suzhou. Each of the many gardens there has its unique style. Visit the Humble Administrator's Garden, the largest in Suzhou, or Lion's Grove, with its specially curated rock displays.

9. Visit the West Lake in Hangzhou, with Its Many Breathtaking Scenes

The West Lake, undisputedly the most famous sight in Hangzhou, is actually composed of many sights. Over the ages, poets and artists have visited the lake and lauded the beauty of each of its "scenes".

BEST OF SHANGHAI ITINERARIES

3 Perfect Days in Shanghai

Day 1

Start with modern Shanghai in Pu Dong District. Pick one of the soaring towers for a panoramic view of the city. Walk through the area, before heading to the Yu Garden. The area has plenty of eating and shopping options along the streets, including the famous soup buns, known as "xiao long bao" in Chinese. Hop over to Xin Tian Di District after dinner and experience the nightlife – plenty of bars and live music.

Day 2

On Day Two, head to People's Square. Spend a few hours looking through the valuable artifacts in Shanghai Museum. Walk along Nanjing Road and experience the bustling city atmosphere. End the day by taking in the nighttime view from the Bund.

Day 3: Day Trip to Hangzhou

Board the speed train to Hangzhou in the morning and head to West Lake right away. Take a West Lake cruise for the most famous sights around here, before visiting Ling Yin Temple. After a lunch of West Lake cuisine, head to Six Harmonies Pagoda. Take the train back to Shanghai at the end of the day.

Alternatively, consider taking a day trip to Suzhou if you're more interested in traditional Chinese gardens or a day trip to one of the water towns near Shanghai, such as Qibao or Zhujiazui, to experience an ancient Chinese village.

Planning to visit Beijing or other cities along with your trip to Shanghai? Check out our China at a Glance Itinerary and Best of China Itinerary below!

China in a Nutshell – 10 Days
Beijing - Xi'an - Shanghai - Hangzhou - Guilin

Day 1 – 3: Beijing

Spend the first day in East City District. Start the morning by snapping some photos in front of Tian'anmen Square, before heading into the massive Forbidden City and admire the living quarters of China's emperors. From there, take a walk to the Temple of Heaven and the Drum and Bell Towers. Afterward, look through the interesting boutique shops along Nan Luo Gu Xiang for unique souvenirs. Have some Peking duck for dinner. If you are up for more, go for a drink lakeside in Hou Hai.

Head to Summer Palace on your second morning and admire the harmony between nature and architecture. Leave the Qing Dynasty for modern China after that, and head to Chaoyang District. You can look at the massive parks that were converted from the 2008 Beijing Olympic structures, visit a few galleries in 798 Art Zone, and shop for antiques in Pan Jia Yuan. End the day in San Li Tun Bar Street.

Reserve your third day in Beijing for the Great Wall. Most go to Ba Da Ling, but for a less crowded location, visit Mu Tian Yu.

For more details on visiting Beijing, find our Comprehensive **Best of Beijing** City Guide.

Days 4 – 5: Xi'an

Spend the morning with the Terracotta Warriors, the world's eighth wonder. In the afternoon, visit the Great Mosque, with its unique mixture of Islamic and Chinese influences. Explore the surrounding Muslim Quarter after for some delicious street food and fun souvenirs.

Walk around the ancient city walls on your second morning in Xi'an, or hire a bike. From there, visit the Big Wild Goose Pagoda. For more history, spend the rest of the day at the Shaanxi History Museum.

Day 6 – 7: Shanghai

Follow the three-day itinerary in Shanghai above.

Days 8: Day Trip to Hangzhou

Follow the day trip itinerary to Hangzhou above.

Days 9: Guilin

Explore the most famous sights in Guilin, including Elephant Trunk Hill and Reed Flute Cave. Be sure to take a photo in front of "Guilin's Scenery Ranks First in the World." Take an evening Li River Cruise from Guilin to Yangshuo.

Day 10: Yangshuo

Explore the picturesque area all around Yangshuo. You can hike or bike through the fresh rural landscape. Later in the day, explore the many expats-run bars and restaurants and chat with someone from a different part of the world.

Have more time? Consider adding Hong Kong, Tibet and Chengdu to your itinerary. For more information on Hong Kong, find our Comprehensive **Best of Hong Kong** City Guide.

SHANGHAI

Orientation to Shanghai
The city is split in two by Huangpu River – the area to the west is called Puxi, while the area to the east is called Pudong. Puxi is the older central part of the city, where the Bund and other attractions from the city's colonial past can be found, while Pudong is the rapidly developing area across the river, where most high-rises and the Special Economic Zone is located.

For this travel guide, Pudong is considered one district, while the larger and older Puxi divided into districts.

See

The Bund

The Bund has been the symbol of Shanghai for as long as the city was around. This famous and attractive stretch of waterfront winds along the west bank of Huangpu River for just under a mile, from Wai Bai Du Bridge to Nan Pu Bridge. Historically, this was one of the most fashionable addresses in Shanghai. Today, tourists flock here to see first and foremost the 26 buildings of various architectural styles including Gothic, Baroque, Romanesque, Classic, and the Renaissance – styles that would not exist side by side anywhere else – from the city's colonial past. There is also the "Lovers' Wall", the flood-control wall located on the side of the Huangpu River between Huang Pu Park to Xin Kai River. In the beginning of the last century, this was once the most romantic spot in Shanghai. While it may be a less intimate date place now, Lovers' Wall still provides a very good view of the Pu Dong Area with its new skyscrapers, distinct from the older style European buildings on the Bund.

Visit the Bund at sunset or after 8pm, and you'll be rewarded with a view far more beautiful than if you come during the daytime. Beware that scammers and prostitutes tend to work this area and target tourists. Avoid contact with both to be safe.

Transit: Take Subway Line 2 to Nanjing East Road. From there, walk 7 minutes west toward the river.

Experience

Skyline Views from the Bund
There are still many fancy restaurants and bars along the Bund, offering stunning nighttime views of the skyline. Here are two favorites of locals and travelers alike:

Bar Rouge
This magnificent dance club and bar gives any venue in Las Vegas a run for its money. A terrace on the 7th floor looks over the Huangpu River and the skyline on the opposite shore. Stylish, very international patrons frequent this glowing red bar, where if you order the signature Bar Rouge drink, they set the bar alight. There are often acrobatic and dance performances, that lend the club a very riotous and festive atmosphere. Surprisingly, Bar Rouge is posh but still quite affordable. The drinks are delicious but won't break the bank. There is a weekly Ladies' Night when ladies get free drinks.

Captain's Bar
Captain's Bar is even more affordable than Bar Rouge, with a distinctly more laidback vibe. Located on the roof of Captain's Hostel, the low-key and welcoming bar is very popular with backpackers, and younger, less pretentious locals. Grab a few pints here and settle in, enjoy the view while you get to know the person sitting next to you.

French Concession

As its name suggests, this area was once designated for French expats in Shanghai during the colonial periods, once known as the Paris of the East. Today, French Concession is one of the richest and most vibrant neighborhoods in the city. Shanghai Stadium, traditional Shi Ku Men Houses, the famous Xu Jia Hui Shopping District, and the former resident of Sun Yat-sen, can all still be found here. Whether you are looking for tourist destinations or just some shopping time, French Concession has plenty to offer.

See

Old French Concession Streets
Wealthy French and Belgians living in Shanghai would have lived on or around Huai Hai Road in the beginning of the 20th century. They left some very pretty houses that both suggest the styles popular in their native countries at the time, and the Chinese aesthetics of the day. Many of those houses are increasingly being turned into trendy designer clothing boutiques. Explore the area between Ju Lu Road to the north and Huai Hai Road running through the center of the area, plus Mao Ming Road to the south of the Huai Hai Road. Walk along broad, pleasantly tree-lined streets and watch for fashionable youngsters hurrying by on their phones.

Transit: Take Subway Line 10 to Xin Tian Di Station.

Sun Yat-sen's Former Residence
The Father of China's Republic, Sun Yat-sen, and his wife, Soong Ching Ling, lived in this house from 1918 to 1937. The house has been converted into a museum in 1961, and tells the story of Sun's life and career.

Transit: Take Subway Line 10 to Xin Tian Di Station. The residence is located at 7 Xiang Shan Road.

Soong Ching Ling's Former Residence

The wife of Sun Yat-sen, Madame Soong Ching Ling was a respected politician in her own right, and took part in the politics of the Communist Party especially after Sun's death. As such, much state business took place here. The house has also been converted into a museum with many artifacts that focus on the politics of China leading up to the founding of the People's Republic of China in 1949. Soong was educated in the U.S. and spoke fluent English, so much of the exhibit should be interesting to Chinese and non-Chinese alike. There are also a few state-used cars in the well-maintained garage on the grounds.

Transit: Take Subway Line 10 or Line 11 to Jiao Tong University Station.

Site of the First National Congress of Communist Party of China

Located next to the fashionable pedestrian area of Xin Tian Di, the Site of the First National Congress of Communist Party of China is more austere and far more historically intriguing. On July 23, 1921, 13 founding members held the very first national congress of the Communist Part of China here, marking the birth of the ruling party today. Since opening 50 years ago, over 10 million visitors from China and abroad have attended the museum. Recent years, the number of visitors has increased dramatically after the museum was remodeled in 1999.

Transit: Take Subway Line 10 to Xin Tian Di Station.

Experience

Xin Tian Di Pedestrian Area

In the 1920's Shanghai, Xin Tian Di area was a predominantly residential area, with many traditional Shi Ku Men houses. Today, you can still admire them with their well-maintained antique walls, intricate tiles and unique exteriors, but on the inside, a different, more modern world occupies these old houses. International galleries, bars, cafes, trendy boutiques, and theme restaurants have found their homes in this historical district, turning it into a famous urban attraction for tourists, cool locals, and expats living in Shanghai. Take a walk around, shop, eat, drink, people watch, and just take in the bustling city atmosphere.

Transit: Take Subway Line 10 to Xin Tian Di Station.

Xu Ja Hui Shopping

You can find everything you need in this massive shopping district. Centered on the intersection of Hong Qiao Road, Hua Shan Road, Zhao Jia Bang Road, and North Cao Xi Road, the district is home to three supermarkets, six major shopping malls, and nine large-scale office towers. Grand Gateway Mall is the poshest of these malls. While you can find anything from groceries to cosmetics here, Xu Jia Hui is most famous for its electronics stores. There is a huge variety of electronic equipment, from cameras to PSPs, Xboxes and other gaming consoles. Pacific Digital Plaza is the place to start. You can easily spend whole days here.

Transit: Take Subway Line 1 to Xu Jia Hui Station.

Old Town

Despite its name, Old Town is not exclusively old, but refers to the area enclosed in the ancient city walls of Shanghai, around Re Min and Zhong Hua Streets today. This district remained exclusively Chinese even during the foreign concessions period.

Foreigners rarely came here in those days. Today, plenty of foreign tourists and expats come here for attractions touted as "old Shanghai", which are picturesque but rather touristy. Venture into side streets for a more authentic old Shanghai feel. Modern skyscrapers have sprang up over recent years, making up a very contradictory but unique landscape.

See

Yu Yuan (Yu Garden)
A famous classical Chinese garden on par with the gardens in Suzhou, a government official of the Ming Dynasty built Yu Yuan in 1577, as a tranquil place for his parents to retire in their old age. Indeed, "Yu" means pleasant and satisfying in Chinese.

Like its counterparts in Suzhou and other cities in this part of China, Yu Garden is laid out thoughtfully with beautiful landscaped scenery set with traditional Chinese architecture. These halls and rooms contain century-old furniture, and are decorated with calligraphy and painting masterpieces. Most think Yu Garden is as exquisite as the Humble Administrator's Garden in Suzhou.

Transit: Take Subway Line 10 to Yu Yuan Station.

Yu Yuan Market
This market next to Yu Garden has over ten shopping streets. It's a good place to bargain for a few souvenirs or sample some well-known local snacks.

Transit: Take Subway Line 10 to Yu Yuan Station.

Temple of the Town God (Cheng Huang Miao)
Most ancient Chinese town, big or small, have a temple dedicated to their town god, used as a place of worship as well as a sort of center of market like the Forum in Ancient Rome. The one in Shanghai, located not far from Yu Garden, is quite impressive – it is the biggest and best-preserved example of traditional Chinese architecture in the city.

There is an old Shanghai saying: one who fails to reach the temple never reaches Shanghai. This is still true today. Locals still visit on holidays to pray for the protection and favor of the gods, while visitors go to the temple and the surrounding areas for both a taste of old Shanghai, and shopping and snacks in the busy streets filled with vendors.

Transit: Take Subway Line 10 to Yu Yuan Station.

Experience

Try Local Snacks and Shop for Local Goods in the Temple of the Town God Area
After 6:30pm, the area surrounding the Temple of the Town God lights up, showing off the ancient beauty of the buildings in a modern way. There are quite a few restaurants to choose from here, including some that overlook the square on Yu Yuan Road – it's a stunning view!

Jing An District

Jing An is one of the oldest districts in Shanghai. It has been inhabited continuously since the 3rd century AD. Today it is home to the old – like the famous Jing An Temple, and the new – like the famous commercial and shopping district of West Nanjing Road, which extends from the middle of Jing An District to People's Square.

See

Jing An Temple (Jing An Si)
Jing An Temple is as famous as the Temple of the Town God and quite deservedly so. Originally built in 247 BC, rebuilt multiple

times in its history, and relocated to its current site in the 1880s, this Buddhist temple is one of the top attractions in Shanghai.

There are three main halls in the temple – Hall of Heavenly Kings, Mahavira Hall, and Three Sage Hall, all filled with religious artifacts, calligraphy, painting, and sculptures from the temple's history. In particular, the massive portrait of the Sakyamuni in Mahavira Hall, measuring 3.78 meters in height, and weighing in at 11,000 kilograms, is known for the tranquil expression of the Buddha pictured – a sort of Mona Lisa of China.

Transit: Take Subway Line 2 or Line 7 to Jing An Temple Station.

People's Square
Here in People's Square is the geographical, political, and cultural heart of modern Shanghai. Bisecting Nanjing Road into East and West, People's Square was once a Colonial-era racecourse known as the "No. 1 Racecourse in the Far East." In 1949, People's Avenue was built across the area, with the square to its south, and People's Park to its north. In 1966, one million Red Guards gathered here. By the time a comprehensive reconstruction finished in 1993, this city center square covered about 140,000 square meters, the biggest public square of the city.

Transit: Take Subway Line 1, 2, 8 to People's Square.

People's Park (Ren Min Park)
Located across People's Avenue from People's Square, the park is a pleasant area that covers a total of 24.3 acres.

There are three sections in the park. In the east, there is the Memorial to the May Thirtieth Movement. In the middle area, you can find the Antarctic Stone, the Shanghai Museum of Contemporary Art, a teahouse, an outdoor theater, and a dance hall. There is also a jungle section where you can have a picnic on the stone stables, or play chess with the locals. In the west, the landscape is pleasantly curated with artificial hills, bodies of water, pergolas, corridors, and pavilions.

The park is also known for its marriage market weekly, see below.

Transit: Take Subway Line 1, 2, 8 to People's Square.

Shanghai Museum
One of the best museums of Chinese art and artifacts anywhere in the world, Shanghai Museum occupies a premiere location in People's Square. The stunning building resembles a bronze urn, highlighting the fact that the museum houses the world's greatest collection of Chinese bronzes. Over 400 pieces of the most exquisite bronze wares to have survived history, mostly from the Shang and Zhou Dynasties, evoke this important period of ancient Chinese art.

In addition to the bronzes, there are galleries dedicated to Ancient Ceramics, Paintings, Calligraphy, Ancient Sculpture, Ancient Jade, Coins, Ming and Qing Furniture, Seals, and Minority Nationalities. All exhibits are well-curated and incorporate state-of-the-art technology in presenting the artifacts artfully in world-class facilities. All information is presented in Chinese and English. The excellent audio guide is also available in both languages.

The bronze ware of the Shang and Zhou dynasties contribute to our understanding of ancient civilization. The over 400 pieces of exquisite bronze wares cover the history of ancient Chinese bronze art.

Transit: Take Subway Line 1, 2, 8 to People's Square.

Nanjing Road

This famous 3.4-mile-long shopping street gives Fifth Avenue, Time Square, and Ginza a run for their money for all its glittering neon lights and world-class shopping. It starts at the Bund in the east, and runs west to the junction of Jing An Temple and Yan An West Street. At the center of the street is also the center point of Shanghai – People's Square.

Shanghai began to develop rapidly after the Opium War. During the concession era, Nanjing Road became alternatively the British Concession, then the International Settlement. With the importing of foreign goods, it quickly became the most fashionable shopping street in the city. In the 1930s, the street was named one of the "World's Seven Great Roads."

After decades of languishing under Communist austerity, the street has more than recovered its former glory since, attracting shoppers and people watchers from every corner of the world. There are over 600 businesses along both sides of the road, including top fashion brands like Chanel and Prada, high street boutiques, and tons of restaurants and food vendors. For those with more old-world tastes, over one hundred traditional stores still stock premium silk goods, jade, embroidery, wool, and clocks.

Sightseers can catch the trackless train for a tour of the pedestrian street, or take a leisurely albeit crowded stroll and look at the sculptures, street musicians, and some of the most fashionable people in the world. At night everything flashes neon lights, transforming the street into an even brighter spectacle.

Transit: Take Subway Line 2 to West Nanjing Road, or Subway Line 1, 2, 8 to People's Square.

Experience

Shanghai Marriage Market in People's Park

Walking by People's Park on a weekend afternoon, you may be attracted by the huge crowd of elderly people all milling about as if at a farmer's market. This is actually a weekly marriage brokering market where mostly desperate parents and grandparents of singles come looking for a mate for their unmarried child.

The Chinese have always had the tradition of choosing a suitable match for their offspring based on a number of criteria including age, height, family upbringing, income and job, mostly through friends and family relationships. This market in Shanghai acts like a dating site in real life – parents write all of the above relevant information about their child in a slip of paper, and hang it on long strings holding up similar advertisements. Afterward, they walk around looking at these papers and talking to other parents, hoping to find a good match for their child.

The "Marriage Market" takes place every Saturday and Sunday afternoon, until about 5pm, at the north end of People's Park.

Pudong District

Across the Huangpu River from the Bund, Pudong is the newest and most modern district in Shanghai. Over the last 15 years, the Special Economic Zone sprang up on farmlands and is today full of futuristic skyscrapers where financial and commercial activities concentrate. Pudong International Airport, where most foreign visitors will fly into, is also in this district.

See

Oriental Pearl TV Tower
Whether locals like it or not, this gaudy pink tower has become a symbol of modern Shanghai. It was built in 1994, and is today the 3rd tallest tower in the world. The design features 11 pink bars on its tip, the 2nd of which features an outdoor viewing platform at 259 meter. Not for the height-phobic, the platform has glass floors

where you can walk onto a transparent path above Pudong and the river. A stunning view and a thrilling adventure wrapped in one! This platform costs ¥100 to experience, while the conventional observation platform in the top ball, at 350 meters high, costs a bit more.

Transit: Take Subway Line 2 to Lu Jia Zui.

Shanghai World Financial Center

The 2nd tallest skyscraper in China, Shanghai World Financial Center (SWFC) was completed in 2008 in the center of the

Special Economic Zone. Three viewing platforms on floors 94, 97, 100 all offer spectacular views of the Bund, the river, and Old Shanghai. Alternatively, the 98 floor has many bars and restaurants, all offering the same view.

Transit: Take Subway Line 2 to Lu Jia Zui.

Jin Mao Tower
Jin Mao, standing just beside Oriental Pearl TV Tower, is the third tallest skyscraper in China. Inside, you'll see a 31-story atrium that rises up like a space station. There is quite a bit you can do here – an Italian restaurant Cucina is located on the 55th floor. You can enjoy a pizza while looking over the Bund and the rest of the opposite bank, for about the same price as going up the Oriental Pearl TV Tower. The 88th floor, the very top floor, also has a restaurant. The Grand Hyatt Shanghai, with Cloud 9 lounge, also offers a grand view, though at quite a price.

Transit: Take Subway Line 2 to Lu Jia Zui.

Experience

Majestic Night Views of the Bund and Old Shanghai from Cloud 9 in Jin Mao Tower
Located on the 87th floor of Jin Mao Tower, Cloud 9 is the highest you can get in a building in Shanghai, higher than the viewing platforms in both Oriental Pearl TV Tower and the SWFC. The view is amazing, but is quite pricey. Note that electricity in buildings on the opposite bank is turned off at 11pm, so the view is less amazing after then.

Transit: Take Subway Line 2 to Lu Jia Zui.

Super Brand Mall (Zheng Da Guang Chang)

This super mall has everything you'd expect – delicious food and shops of every variety. There is a flagship UNIQLO, a Toys 'R' Us, and Ding Tai Fung, which New York Times rated as one of the ten best restaurants in the world.

Transit: Take Subway Line 2 to Lu Jia Zui.

Water Towns near Shanghai

Qi Bao Ancient Town

There are a few ancient water towns with Venice-like canals around Shanghai, but Qi Bao is most conveniently located on the outskirts of the city, and accessible by the Shanghai subway system.

The town dates back to the Northern Song Dynasty, around 960AD. During the Ming and Qing Dynasties, it prospered into a business center with a lively economy. Today, the town is quite small, covering only around two square kilometers, but it is an open air museum of Chinese history in the region. Two canals bisect the small town, where there are many traditional houses that have partially been converted into shops and restaurants. Prices in Qi Bao are cheaper compared to the more touristy water towns, and you'll likely run into fewer crowds here.

Transit: Take Subway Line 9 to Qi Bao Station.

Zhu Jia Jiao

The oldest archaeological sites in this water town date to 5,000 years ago, but it first became a real town around 1,700 years ago. Since then, Zhu Jia Jiao became a trading hub during the Ming and Qing Dynasties. Many waterside buildings, bridges across the canals, and other structures from that time still remain today, making it one of the most well preserved water towns on the outskirts of Shanghai.

The town occupies about three square kilometers with plenty to see. You can see how goods are ferried in the old days, in three boats along the ferries from house to house, passing under one of the 36 stone bridges. There are also ample historical buildings for you to explore, including rice shops, clothing shops, banks, spice stores, and even a Qing-era post office. In particular, Fangsheng Bridge, Kezhi Garden, and the Yuanjin Buddhist Temple make for a very interesting visit and beautiful pictures.

Even though Zhu Jia Jiao has become a popular destination, you can walk around to some back alleys where locals still live, mostly elderlies and artists here for the authentic water town atmosphere. When you are tired from walking along the attractive streets, stop by one of the teahouses, coffeehouses, bars, and restaurants in town, many of which overlook the water.

Getting Here
Taking a bus from the Pu An Lu bus station near People's Square, or the bus station at Shanghai Ti Yu Guan, is the most affordable way to reach Zhu Jia Jiao.

Zhou Zhuang

About one and a half hours out of Shanghai, and closer to Suzhou, Zhou Zhuang is the most famous and popular of the water towns in the area. One look at the well preserved roofs sloping over the elegant canals, and you can easily see why the town is so popular with visitors. You can take a ferryboat around the network of waterways, and take in the most attractive of the old dwellings built during the Ming and Qing Dynasties. There are also many shops that have become quite famous in their own right for their folk art and crafts. We recommend staying overnight in Zhou Zhuang, and taking advantage of early mornings, when the town is at its most peaceful. During the weekends, it can get very crowded. Buses run to Zhou Zhuang from Suzhou and Shanghai.

What to Eat in Shanghai

Shanghai, just like Beijing, has food from everywhere in China and the rest of the world, but its local cuisine certainly gives the imports a run for their money. Traditional Shanghai cuisine is relatively young compared to other major cuisines in China, originating in the Ming Dynasty, around 15th century, but underwent important updates under the influences of other cuisines when the city became an international trading hub. Shanghai cuisine makes full use of its location on the river, which floats into the Yellow Sea, with plenty of freshwater fish, seafood, and special water plants. The emphasis is on the freshness and lightness of the raw materials, and the artful arrangement of each dish. Shanghai food is also usually sweet, as sugar is an important ingredient, and often marinated or cooked in wine, which is called "drunken"-style cooking.

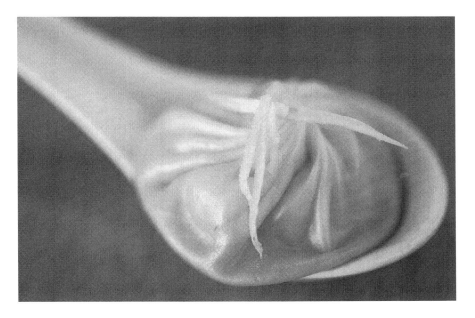

Soup Buns

Soup buns, or "xiao long bao" in Chinese, are world famous. These delicate little buns contain meat and crab roe filling from Shanghai hairy crabs, with a hot, richly flavored stock that comes dripping out as soon as you bite into it. The trick is that the stock is cooled into a gelatin texture, and filled into the buns along with the meat. The heat from the steamer melts the stock again, for you drink straight out of the bun.

Almost all Shanghainese restaurants will have soup buns on the menu, but the undisputed most famous soup bun restaurant is Nan Xiang, near the Temple of the City God and Yu Garden. The restaurant has more than 100 years of history, and provides an authentic dining experience in addition to the delicious buns. First floor is for takeaways; second floor is for casual diners, while the third floor is a nice sit-down restaurant.

Address: Nan Xiang Xiaolong Mantou, 85 Yuyuan Old Road.

Sheng Jian Bao
A bun only slightly less famous than soup buns is called "**sheng jian bao**", which is a lot sturdier and just as delicious. Thick-skinned pork buns are pan-fried until the bottom is crispy. The best place to grab some of these for a snack is Yang's Fried Dumpling.

Address: 269 Wujiang Road.

Hairy Crabs
These popular crabs can only be found in autumn, so if you find them during other seasons, chances are they are fake. But during the fall, do not miss the decadent crustaceans, especially the crab roe, which the Chinese love.

Try Tongchuan Seafood Market with its many vendors. You can purchase fresh seafood from a stall, and then ask a restaurant to cook them up. Locals eat these steamed to appreciate the fresh subtle flavor.

Address: No. 5, 928 Tongchuan Road.

Green Onion Pancakes

These flaky fried pancakes are called "cong you bing" in Chinese, and they are delicious! Restaurants offer them as appetizers, but if you want to be a local, get up early and look in the city's many small streets for stalls run by grannies, who start frying these up before the sun rises, just in time for locals who want to grab a quick breakfast before heading to work. Follow your nose!

Fried Noodles

If you are at loss as to what to order at a Shanghainese restaurant, fried noodles are a pretty safe way to go. These are not your average "chow mein" at the Chinese restaurants back at home, but amazing fresh thick noodles, stir fried with meat, chicken, or shrimps, soy sauce, and plenty of oil. The result is a slick and flavorful dish that is great by itself or complementing other dishes. Try Ming Ming Restaurant for this local favorite.

Address: 269 Beihai Road.

Best Areas to Stay in Shanghai

Around The Bund
Staying in a hotel along the Bund should offer you a breathtaking view of the Huangpu River at night. During the day, you'll have easy access to public transportations to almost all famous attractions like Yu Garden, Jing'an Temple, Shanghai Museum, and Nanjing Road.

East Nanjing Road
Connected to the rest of the city by Subway Lines 2 and 10, the eastern stretch of Nanjing Road has tons of shopping and lots of good food all around. An added advantage is the Bund being within walking distance along Nanjing Road.

French Concession near Xu Jia Hui
If you stay in Xu Jia Hui area, you won't have to go far for anything. The picturesque French Concession is close by, and there are also many shopping, eating, and going out options. The area is considerably less touristy than Nanjing Road and the Bund, so you'll be more likely to run into locals wherever you go. Subway Lines 1, 10, and 11 connect to the rest of the city.

Pudong near Lu Jia Zui
The sparkling new financial district in Pudong is very modern with almost all of Shanghai's most famous skyscrapers – Oriental Pearl TV Tower, International Financial Center, Jinmao Tower, and Lu Jia Zui Trade and Financial Center – and the hotels are just as new and swanky as well. Try to stay near the Lu Jia Zui Subway Station though, to shorten your trip to other sights in Old Shanghai, across the Yangtze River.

Shanghai Nightlife

Bund Area
There are tons of bars of every price range in the Bund, many with a view over the river and nighttime Shanghai.

Bar Rouge

This magnificent dance club and bar gives any venue in Las Vegas a run for its money. A terrace on the 7th floor looks over the Huangpu River and the skyline on the opposite shore. Stylish, very international patrons frequent this glowing red bar, where if you order the signature Bar Rouge drink, they set the bar alight. There are often acrobatic and dance performances, that lend the club a very riotous and festive atmosphere. Surprisingly, Bar Rouge is posh but still quite affordable. The drinks are delicious but won't break the bank. There is a weekly Ladies' Night when ladies get free drinks.

Address: Bund 18, 7/F, 18 Zhongshan Dong Yi Road

Captain's Bar

Captain's Bar is even more affordable than Bar Rouge, with a distinctly more laidback vibe. Located on the roof of Captain's Hostel, the low-key and welcoming bar is very popular with backpackers, and younger, less pretentious locals. Grab a few pints here and settle in, enjoy the view while you get to know the person sitting next to you.

Address: No. 37 Fuzhou Road

M1NT
M1NT is a posh venue, with lounge, club, and restaurant combined into one on the top floor of a skyscraper near the Bund. The view is as good as any from the towers in Pudong, and fancier with shark tanks and a swanky interior. Chinese and expat of every age group love this place. You'll find younger people on the dance floor, while older and wealthier clientele can be found at one of the tables in the lounge. Definitely call ahead to reserve a table, or consider purchasing a membership card, if you want to be guaranteed entrance into this exclusive venue.

Address: 24/F, 318 Fuzhou Road

French Concession
International crowds hang out in the French Concession just as they did in the colonial era, as the area is still home to many uniquely themed bars. Many of these venues host special events, so be sure to check their websites – anything from Oktoberfest to Halloween is celebrated here, since there are expats from everywhere in the world here.

Zapata's
One of the most popular bars in Shanghai, and the center of the Hengshan Road night scene, Zapata's is hopping any night of the week. Music is fairly mainstream – rock, pop, and hip hop hits. Wednesday night is ladies' night. Bartenders pour tequila shots directly in your mouth if you are willing to dance on top of the bar. There is a Tex-Mex restaurant upstairs too when you get hungry.

Address: 5 Hengshan Road

The Apartment

Walking into the Apartment, you might think you are in a Soho loft in New York. The lounge has a posh but relaxed atmosphere with a large group sitting area where you can order drinks and shared appetizers, and a smaller dining room with a full menu. There is also a rooftop that overlooks the city.

Address: 3/F, 47 Yongfu Road

Dada

Younger locals and expats love Dada for its unpretentious environment and comfortable atmosphere. Drinks are cheaper than many venues in this area, but there is still a good lounge area, and different music every night with a spacious dance floor. Take advantage of cheap drinks and deals on draft beer.

Address: 115 Xingfu Road

Getting In and Out

By Air
Shanghai is a major travel hub for China and Greater Asia. There are two airports: Pudong International Airport, where most foreigners will fly into, and Hongqiao Airport, which serves mostly domestic flights. Be sure to check ahead of time where your flight departs.

Between the two airports, you can take a cab for about an hour, or take the cheaper shuttle buses. It is also possible to take Subway Line 2, which connects the two airports at opposite ends. The subway ride takes about two hours.

Pudong International Airport
The main international airport is located 25 miles outside the city. Arrivals are on the first floor, while departures are on the third. The airport is very sleek and modern, with all the amenities you'd expect to find in a major hub.

From Pudong Airport, take Subway Line 2 to city center, where you can connect to other lines and stations. A taxi to People's Square in city center costs about ¥160. Additionally, between 11pm and 5am, there is a 35% price hike.

Hongqiao International Airport
This airport only serves a few international flights – Tokyo Haneda, Seoul Gimpo, Hong Kong, Macau, and Taipei Songshan. Otherwise, domestic flights will likely get in here.

Subway Lines 2 and 10 take you into city center. Alternatively, you can take a cab for around ¥60, which takes you to People's Square in about half an hour.

By Train

Shanghai is a major train hub as well. There are four stations you will likely use.

Shanghai Railway Station (Shanghai Zhan)
This is Shanghai's oldest train station, serving some high-speed trains, in particular, a connection to Hong Kong. You can reach this station on Subway Lines 1, 3, and 4.

Shanghai Hongqiao Railway Station
This enormous and modern station, located in the same complex as Hongqiao Airport, serves high-speed trains to Beijing, Suzhou, Hangzhou, Nanjing, and Tianjin, among other major Chinese cities. It is on Subway Lines 2 and 10, one stop beyond Hongqiao Airport.

Shanghai South Railway Station
This station serves trains to and from the south, except high-speed trains and trains to Hong Kong. It is on Subway Lines 1 and 3.

Shanghai West Railway Station
This station is smaller, and serves some high-speed trains to the direction of Nanjing. There are also a few connector trains to Shanghai Station.

Getting Around in Shanghai

Subway
The Shanghai Subway System is one of the best in the world. Over 14 lines take you everywhere in Shanghai and the surrounding areas. The trains are very new, with English signs everywhere for the convenience of foreign visitors. You can buy a reloadable card for a ¥20 deposit. The reload machines take ¥50 and ¥100 notes.

Bus

The bus is cheaper and even more extensive than the subway. The route numbers beginning with 3 are night buses that run past 11pm, when the subway system closes. However, they are slower. Information at bus stops are in Chinese only, but announcements on the buses are available in English.

SUZHOU

The city of Suzhou is as beautiful as a classical Chinese painting, with ample water running through the city, and stunningly arranged classical gardens that line the canals. In 1997, the classical gardens were inscribed on the UNESCO World Heritage List.

This ancient city dates back to the Kingdom of Wu, from the 12th to the 4th century BC, before even the time of the first emperor of China. After the kingdom was conquered, the city continued to be the center of the Wu culture, which flourished in these parts.

Today, Suzhou is a core city of the Yangtze River Delta Economic Zone. It is an epicenter of China's silk production and trade as it was in ancient China, and its beautiful canals and tranquil gardens continue to inspire scholars, artists, craftsmen, and travelers every day.

A rectangular canal known as the Weichang River, or Weichang He in Chinese binds downtown Suzhou, composed of Canglang, Pingjiang, and part of Jinchang Districts. Most of the major tourist destinations are within its limits.

See

Suzhou's Classical Chinese Gardens
Suzhou is renowned worldwide for its classical Chinese gardens that are each like a piece of art. Aristocrats and other wealthy businessmen have been building these delicate private residences since the 6th century BC, but their designs underwent a particularly artful phase during the Ming Dynasty, from the 14th to the 17th century. In the subsequent Qing Dynasty, these gardens became more prevalent, spreading across the city and its suburbs.

At its core, the architectural philosophy of these gardens strives to recreate nature on a miniature scale. Therefore, the residential part of the garden exists in beautiful harmony with the ponds, rockeries, flowers, and trees, all designed to exhibit Chinese philosophy and ideology. Each small plot of land is carefully curated to evoke grander locales, like mountains and natural springs. Shielded from the bustling city outside by high walls, these gardens are meant to be tranquil havens for their masters, and evoke for visitors today the forgotten elegance of the old China.

Many of these gardens have been restored close to their former glory. The following are the most famous and popular ones in Suzhou.

The Humble Administrator's Garden (Zhuo Zheng Yuan)

Zhuo Zheng Yuan, covering about 12.85 acres, is the largest of the preserved gardens in Suzhou. If you only visit one garden in Suzhou, this would be the one. The garden is renowned for its unique designs and ethereal beauty, and has garnered many honors, including a World Cultural Heritage Site, a Cultural Relic of National Importance under the Protection of the State, and a Special Tourist Attraction of China. It is also considered one of the four most famous gardens in China.

Though its name nods to its master's aspiration to remain a humble servant of the emperor, this garden is anything but humble. Originally built in 1509, during the Ming Dynasty, it took over 16 years to construct, and was said to have cost a boatload of silver to complete.

Transit: Take bus no. 40 or 313, and get off at Bei Yuan Lu Station.

The Garden of the Master of the Nets (Wang Shi Yuan)
A small but infinitely intricate complex, the Garden of the Master of the Nets dates back to 1140 in the Song Dynasty, and was recreated in 1770. Even though it is the smallest of the preserved gardens in Suzhou, you can easily spend half a day or more here, since the artful use of space creates the illusion that the space is much larger than its actual size. On some evenings, you can catch a traditional performance here.

Transit: take bus no. 55, 202, 529, 811 or 931 and get off at Wang Shi Yuan Station

The Lingering Garden (Liu Yuan)
Considered one of the four most famous gardens in China along with the Humble Administrator's Garden, the Lingering Garden is a prominent example of the Qing Dynasty aesthetic, and one of the most stunning classical gardens in Suzhou. It covers 5.8 acres outside the original city gate, and is known for its magnificent

halls with a range of splendid colors. It became a UNESCO World Heritage Site in 1997.

Transit: Take bus no. 34, 44, 45, 85, 161, 311, 406, 933, 949, or Tourism Bus No. 1 to Liu Yuan Station.

The Lion Grove Garden (Shi Zi Lin)
More than other gardens in Suzhou, the Lion Grove Garden is renowned for its array of pitted, eroded rocks that are beautifully arranged, almost like natural, large-scale sculptures. Together, these rocks used to be part of a Buddhist monastery, and in the garden make up a small maze with many twists and turns that children will enjoy exploring.

Transit: Take bus no. 529, 811 or Tourism Bus No.1, 2, & 5, to Suzhou Museum Station.

Suzhou Museum
The Suzhou Museum contains over 15,000 artifacts, including many prized ancient calligraphy, paintings, and other artifacts unearthed in Suzhou and nearby areas. In particular, the porcelain bowls are stunningly restored, and the splendid antique Chinese gowns will make any modern fashionista envious with their luxurious fabrics and intricate craftsmanship.

World-renowned architect, I.M. Pei, who also designed the glass pyramid outside the Louvre in Paris, among many other works across the U.S, specially designed the building. While Pei lived in America for most of his life, his family actually came from Suzhou. To pay respect to his hometown, Pei came out of retirement in his 80s to create this museum that showcases both his modernist sensibility, and the architectural influence and sophisticated taste of this region. The recreated scholar's study is a highlight of the museum.

The museum is free to visit.

Transit: Take bus no. 529, 811 or Tourism Bus No.1, 2, & 5, to Suzhou Museum Station.

Tiger Hill and Tiger Hill Pagoda
The hill, also known as Surging Sea Hill, covers just over three acres of land, and is 118 feet in height. Though the area is relatively small, it is rich in interesting historical sites that date all the way back to the founding of Suzhou, over 2,500 years ago.

The most famous of the Tiger Hill sites is the Tiger Hill Pagoda, which stands at the summit of the hill, as a part of the Yun Yan Temple. It is the oldest pagoda in Suzhou and the surrounding areas, dating back to the Northern Song Dynasty in the 10th century. It has become known as the "Leaning Tower of China", for its incline similar to the Leaning Tower of Pisa in Italy. Its seven-story octahedron shape, measuring over 150 feet high, is constructed in the style of the timber pagodas characteristic of the early Tang Dynasty.

Transit: Take bus no. 32 or express line 3 and get off at Hu Qiu Bei Men (North Gate of Tiger Hill).

Cold Mountain Temple (Hanshan Temple)

In A Night Mooring near Maple Bridge, a famous Tang Dynasty poem, the poet Zhang Ji describes the midnight bells of the Hanshan Temple, and evokes beautifully the tranquil ancient surroundings of the temple. Since then, the temple has become a popular tourist destination even in ancient China, renowned for its bells and the Buddhist culture. The temple was originally constructed in the Liang Dynasty, in the 6th century, but most of the buildings you see today date from the Tang Dynasty in the 7th century.

Maple Bridge, or Feng Qiao, as described in the poem, is located next to the temple. There is also a statue of the poet nearby, as well as shops selling souvenirs related to both the temple and the bridge.

Transit: Take the special Tourism Bus No.3 (You3 Bus) to Lai Feng Qiao.

Experience

Shan Tang Street

This recently-restored canal street runs from Chang Men, the ancient city gate, to Tiger Hill. It winds along the Shan Tang River for about 2.2 miles or seven "li" – seven Chinese miles, hence the nickname "Seven-Li Shan Tang". The pedestrian street offers a nice stroll, with local snack and souvenir vendors along both sides. While the southeast end of the street close to the city gates may be crowded with tourists, stalls, and touristy restaurants, the northern end is quieter and much nicer for a leisurely walk. It also passes through some local residential neighborhoods, so you'll have a chance to glimpse into how the locals live.

You can also take a river cruise at various points along the walk, to experience the city from the water.

Transit: Take Subway Line 2 to Shantang Street Station.

What to Eat

Suzhou is known for its fish dishes, made with fresh fish from the lake, cooked more delicately compared to in northern China. In particular, try "**Squirrel-Shaped Fish**", or Song Shu Yu, which is a lightly fried whole deboned fish, dressed in a sweet and sour sauce, or **Whitebait Soup**, which is made with a small, smooth fish, bamboo shoots, and vegetables. Other dishes in traditional Suzhou cuisine are just as carefully prepared. Expect subtle but nuanced flavors.

Getting In and Out

By Air
Suzhou does not have its own commercial airport. Most travelers fly into Shanghai, and travel by train to Suzhou. The airport in the city of Wuxi is closer, but serves mostly domestic flights. Nanjing and Hangzhou are other options.

By Train
Suzhou Station (Suzhou Zhan)
Just north of downtown, Suzhou Station is a stop on the Shanghai-Nanjing train line. There are frequent high-speed connections to Shanghai, Wuxi, Changzhou, Zhenjiang, and Nanjing. A high-speed "G-train" takes you to Shanghai in less than half an hour, and Nanjing in an hour. There are also slower T- and K- trains at this station to and from other provinces.

Suzhou North Railway Station (Suzhou Bei Zhan)
This station, located on the outskirts of the city, serves high-speed trains to and from Beijing, which only takes about five hours.

By Bus
Three inter-city bus terminals in Suzhou offer regular shuttles to Shanghai, Nanjing, Hangzhou, and other major destinations around China.

Getting Around in Suzhou

Subway
The one functioning subway line runs east west between New District, Old Town, and Suzhou Industrial Park. A second line is under construction.

Bus
The extensive bus lines cover the entire city, and run at 10 to 20 minute internals between 5am and 9pm on most routes. They are

quite affordable. All information and announcements are in Chinese only, but you can search on Google Maps ahead of time to plan your travel.

HANGZHOU

The city of Hangzhou, located at the southern terminus of the Grand Canal and on the lower reaches of the Qiantang River, was the capital city of the Southern Song Dynasty from 1127, until Mongols overran it in 1276. At the time, with as many as one million inhabitants, Hangzhou was the largest city in the world, and so grand that Marco Polo called it "beyond dispute the finest and the noblest in the world".

Today, Hangzhou is one of the most popular tourist destinations in China. Its subtropical monsoon climate makes the city variedly beautiful in each season. As such, the West Lake, the city's most renowned landmark, has been lauded throughout history for its scenes in different seasons.

See

West Lake Area

West Lake (Xi Hu)
The beauty of the West Lake has inspired poets, artists, and lovers throughout Chinese history. This most scenic and famous of lakes in Hangzhou is surrounded by mountains on three sides, and divided into five inner lakes – the North Inner Lake, the Yuehu Lake, the West Inner Lake, the South Lake, and the West Outer Lake by the three causeways named after famous Chinese poets – the Bai Causeway, the Su Causeway, and the Yang Causeway. There are several large natural islands, as well as a few man-made islands that dot the vast lake district.

During the Qing Dynasty, Emperor Kangxi, who visited West Lake a few times, came up with 10 Scenes of the West Lake – 10 most scenic spots of the area in a season during which it is most beautiful, like "Snowfall over Broken Bridge." He later added 10 more called 10 New Scenes of the West Lake. We highlight a few of the top scenes below.

Transit: Take Subway Line 1 to Long Xiang Qiao. Upon arrival, walk westward to reach the Lakeside Park (Music Fountain) or northward to Broken Bridge or Bai Causeway.

Alternatively, take the same subway to Ding'an Road. Upon arrival, walk westward to lakeside Nanshan Mountain area or southward to Wushan Mountain area.

Dawn on the Su Causeway in Spring

Constructed under the guidance of and named after the great Song Dynasty poet Su Dongpo, the Su Causeway stretches over 1.7 miles, and includes six beautiful bridges along its length: the Crossing Rainbow Bridge, the Eastern lakeside Bridge, the Suppressing Dike Bridge, the Viewing Hills Bridge, the Locking Waves Bridge, and the Reflecting Ripples Bridge. As the name of the scene suggests, this causeway is most breathtaking in the spring, when the willow trees that line its entirety become a fresh green, and the peach trees bear pink blossoms. At dawn, everything is bathed in gold. It is quite worth getting up in the dark if you are up for it.

Winery Yard and Lotus Pool in Summer

In the Southern Song Dynasty, there was a winery at this spot in the northwest section of the lake that in the summer would be surrounded by lotus flowers in the lake around it. The intoxicating aroma of wine mixed with the fragrance of lotus flowers and together, carried by the gentle lakeside breeze, reached unsuspecting visitors for miles.

There is much to be appreciated at a single scenic spot here, including Yuehu Lake, the Bamboo Garden, the Lakeside Woods, the Winery Yard, and the Lotus Pool. You can sample imperial wine while looking over the stunning summer lotus flowers, or take a walk through the beautiful gardens characteristic of southern China.

Lingering Snow on the Broken Bridge in Winter
The famous Broken Bridge is actually famously not broken. Situated at the foot of the Precious Stone Hill to the eastern end of the Bai Causeway, the bridge is named for the view of it from the hill after snow: snow in the middle section of the bridge melts first, while snow at either ends linger a while longer, causing the illusion that the bridge is broken in the middle. The remaining white snow glistens in the sunshine.

Moon over the Peaceful Lake in Autumn
For the traditional Chinese Mid-Autumn Festival, there is no better place to appreciate the glorious full moon than the West Lake, specifically at the Peaceful Lake to the west of the Bai Causeway. There is an octagonal pavilion at the spot, a platform over the lake, and some other buildings, all constructed for admiring the full moon. Chinese literary luminaries over the ages have left their tributes to the same full moon, which can now be seen in the Xi Ling Calligraphy and Painting Gallery, also at this spot.

Lei Feng Pagoda in Evening Glow
The famous pagoda, standing on the Lei Feng Peak of the Sunset Hill to the south of the West Lake, is the first colorful branze pagoda in China. The top of the pagoda offers a stunning view of the nearby Jing Ci Temple, the landscapes of the West Lake, and even the city of Hangzhou in the distance. In the evening, the late sun casts its golden lights on the colorful pagoda and the green mountains, both reflected in the rippling lake.

Other Areas in Hangzhou

Temple of Soul's Retreat (Ling Yin Temple)
There are two peaks to the northwest of the West Lake – Peak Flown from Afar, and North Peak. In the narrow valley between

them is the Temple of Soul's Retreat, one of the three oldest and most famous temples in China. The monastery dates back to 328 AD, during the Eastern Jin Dynasty. Its founder is a legendary monk from India known as Hui Li.

Aside from the temple, there are a large number of grottos and religious rock carvings that are worth admiring. All together, there are hundreds of Buddhist stone statues carved directly into these cliffs.

Transit: Take Tourism Bus No. 1 (Y1), Tourism Bus No. 2 (Y2), 7/K7, Y13, K807/K837 to Ling Yin Temple Station.

Six Harmonies Pagoda (Liu He Pagoda)

This stunning masterpiece of ancient Chinese architecture sits atop Yue Lun Hill, overlooking Qian Tang River and the southern tip of the West Lake. The pagoda is octagonal in shape, and appears to have 13 stories when seen from the outside. Interestingly though, on the inside, there are only seven stories. You can count them! A spiral staircase leads to the top of the pagoda. Each story has an elaborate carved and painted ceiling made up of animals, flowers, birds, and characters from Chinese myths.

After climbing the pagoda, head to the nearby park where you can find hundreds of models of the world's most famous pagodas, complete with miniature trees to scale.

Transit: Take K808, K599, 504, Tourism Bus No. 5 to Liu He Pagoda.

Experience

He Fang Ancient Street (He Fang Jie)

This ancient street allows you to experience the historical and cultural character of Hangzhou firsthand. You can find an amazing array of interesting storefronts along its length, including shops showcasing a variety of Chinese crafts like hand-blown sugar candy, paper-cutting, and hand-made dough figurines, and vendors selling local snacks like roasted walnuts and "dragon-whisker" candy. There are also art hawkers, fabric shops, caricaturists, bonsai shops, teahouses and many small eateries.

Walk around the West Lake
The entire lake would take about five hours to walk around at a leisurely pace. The causeways cut through it if you feel like taking a short cut. There are also small non-motor powered boats you can hire for ¥120/hour to take you around the lake and the two main islands.

Spend an Afternoon at a Tea House.

Hangzhou is famous for its production of Long Jing, the most famous green tea in China, so be sure to find a teahouse and sample some locally grown teas while you are here. You can also visit nearby villages known for their tea farms – Man Jue Long Village, Long Jing Village, or Mei Jia Wu Village. They have been developed for tourism over the last two or three years, and can be quite crowded on the weekends with tourists, but during the week or the offseason, you can still spend a tranquil afternoon here watching farmers pick tealeaves.

What to Eat

Hangzhou Cuisine is known for being fresh and relatively sweet, but perhaps a bit heartier compared to dishes from Suzhou. Try **Dongpo Pork**, which is made with thick pieces of pork stewed in a rich sauce, or the interestingly named **Beggar's Chicken**, which is quite tender and delicious. For a lighter dish, try **Shrimps with Dragon Well Green Tea**, the best green tea in China.

Getting In and Out

By Air
Hangzhou Xiaoshan International Airport serves domestic flights from Beijing and Hong Kong, and international flights from Amsterdam, Delhi, Kuala Lumpur, Tokyo, Osaka, Bangkok, Seoul, and Singapore. From other foreign cities, you can fly into airports in Shanghai, as Hangzhou is just a short train ride away.

From the airport, you can take an airport shuttle for ¥20, which takes you into the city in around an hour.

By Train
High-speed G- or D- trains connect Hangzhou to Shanghai Hongqiao Station in around 50 minutes non-stop, for about ¥78. Trains with a few stops take around 60 minutes. Trains also run to Guangzhou, Beijing, Chengdu, and other major Chinese cities from Hangzhou.

By Bus
Four inter-city bus terminals in Suzhou offer regular shuttles to Shanghai, Nanjing, Suzhou, and other major destinations around China.

Getting Around in Hangzhou

Subway
There is only one line currently.

Bus
The bus is a good and affordable alternative to traveling by taxi, which is notoriously expensive. The bus announcements and information is all in Chinese, but you can use Google Maps,

which is very accurate for the city, ahead of time or on your phone to find directions and track your location.

PLANNING YOUR TRIP

Climate and Best Time to Visit Shanghai

The region in which Shanghai is located is on the mouth of the Yangtze River where it meets the East China Sea. This makes the area very wet – it rains for about a third of the year. Other than that, the weather in Shanghai is mild with four distinct seasons. Spring and fall are the best seasons to visit, as they are cool and pleasant. In the spring, flowers are in bloom all over the city, making your pictures particularly attractive. There are occasional light showers that should not disturb your plans too much.

Summer is humid and rainy. July and August are the hottest time of the year, with more than 10 days on average above 95 degrees Fahrenheit (35 degrees Celsius). Winter is quite chilly and overcast, with notoriously poor heating, with an average low of just 34 degrees Fahrenheit (1 degree Celsius).

Suzhou and Hangzhou have similar climates to Shanghai.

Holidays/Festivals

There are five major holidays in China, during which time the Chinese travel very heavily. As a result, try to avoid traveling during these days so you don't have to deal with very crowded trains and flights, as well as attractions.

Chinese New Year
Also known as Spring Festival, Chinese New Year is usually in late January to mid-February, depending on the Chinese lunar calendar. This is a very busy and hectic time in China. It is the

longest holiday in China, and traditionally a time for returning to one's extended family. Nearly the entire city will be shut down, so you'd be hard pressed to find anything to do or eat then. In addition, everyone will be trying to go home, making it the absolute worst time to take trains or flights, unless you are up to dealing with Chinese crowds.

Qing Ming Festival
Usually on April 4th to 6th, Qing Ming is the traditional tomb-sweeping day for the Chinese to pay respect to their ancestors. Cemeteries and other locations outside the city tend to be very crowded, and traffic out to the city will be very bad.

Chinese Labor Day
This is a weeklong holiday around May 1st, where many Chinese will be traveling. Try to avoid for sightseeing.

Dragon Boat Festival
Usually in May or June depending on the lunar calendar, this is a festival for boat races and eating "Zong Zi", steamed sticky rice in a pouch made of leaves.

Mid-Autumn Day
Taking place on the 15th day of the 8th lunar month, Mid-Autumn Day is usually in late September or early October. People gather outside to admire the full moon, while eating traditional moon cakes.

National Day and Golden Week
On Oct.1st and the following week, this holiday celebrates the founding of People's Republic of China. Nearly everyone will be traveling during this week, just like Chinese New Year, but usually to visit tourist destinations instead of their families. As such, this is a bad time to travel for tourists.

Early July and Late August
This is not a holiday, but rather when more than 20 million university students go home at the beginning of their summer vacation, and in late August, when they return to school. Trains and flights will be very jammed. It'll be hard to even get tickets.

EXCHANGE RATES

In Mainland China, the currency is called Ren Min Bi (RMB), with the unit of "yuan", denoted by the symbol ¥.

The following rates are calculated at the time of this writing. Please check before your departure for the up-to-date exchange rate.

USD: 1 Dollar = 6.36 Yuan
Canadian Dollar: 1 Canadian Dollar = 4.79 Yuan
British Pounds: 1 Pound = 9.66 Yuan
Euro: 1 Euro = 7.13 Yuan
Australian Dollar: 1 Dollar = 4.46 Yuan

VISA INFORMATION

It is very important to note that visas to Mainland China, and those to Hong Kong and Macau, must be applied separately. Most western visitors will not need visas to visit Hong Kong or Macau, but almost everyone will need a visa to visit Mainland China. Both types can be obtained through a Chinese embassy or consulate. There is an additional permit for foreigners wishing to visit Tibet.

There are a few classes of visas to China: L Visa, for tourists, F Visa, for business trips, exchanges, and study trips, and X Visa for students. The tourist L Visa is quite easy to obtain, and you can apply for single, double, or multiple entries. Single-entry visa is usually valid for 30 days and must be used within three months of issuing. Of course, whether you are granted each type is up to the consulate's discretion.

For more information on specific requirements for the visa application, find more information here: http://www.china-embassy.org/eng/visas/hrsq. For most applicants, a number of documents are required with the application, so be sure to prepare adequately before going to an embassy.

72-Hours Free Transit
To help make international visitors' short stays in China, a number of large cities have adopted this policy to allow passengers carrying passports from 51 countries, including but are not limited to the U.S., Canada, UK, and Schengen region countries, to stay up to 72 hours without a visa on direct transit. The cities include Beijing, Shanghai, Guangzhou, Chengdu, Chongqing, Harbin, Shenyang, Dalian, Xi'an, Guilin, Kunming, Wuhan, Xiamen, Tianjin, and Hangzhou.

Tibet Travel Permit

All non-Chinese citizens must apply for a Tibet Travel Permit, issued by the Tibet Tourism Bureau. For any trains, flights, or buses headed to Tibet, this permit will be checked before you are allowed to board.

The only way to obtain this permit is by arranging for a tour operated by an approved Tibetan travel agent, and the package must include accommodations and transportation. This is important as foreigners are not allowed to take public buses across Tibet, and from the time of landing in Tibet, must travel by private transportation arranged by the tour. Generally, tour groups will have more specific information for applying for this permit, and help you with the process.

Hong Kong Visa

The immigration system to Hong Kong is separate from that of Mainland China, as well as Macau. There are border checks between these three regions. In addition, leaving the Mainland for Hong Kong counts as leaving China. So, if you visit Mainland China first, go to Hong Kong, and want to return to the Mainland, make sure you have a multiple-entry visa to the Mainland, otherwise you will not be able to return. All visitors are also required to demonstrate evidence of adequate funds, and have confirmed booking for the onward journey.

Full citizens of United Kingdom are allowed to visit Hong Kong for 180 days without a visa. Citizens of British Overseas Territories, all EU member states, United States, Canada, and Australia, can visit Hong Kong for 90 days without a visa. For more information, visit http://www.immd.gov.hk/eng/services/visas/visit-transit/visit-visa-entry-permit.html.

HOW TO GET BY - ESSENTIAL CHINESE CULTURE TO KNOW

Chinese culture will likely be quite a shock to western visitors. Some normal local behaviors might prove a bit jarring, but mostly these are not serious problems.

For example, people with obviously non-Chinese features will be considered exotic, and curious locals will stare, or in some cases, ask to take a photo together. Some foreigners might be greeted with a "hello" regardless of where they are from, or are referred to as "laowai", a somewhat affectionate term for "foreigners". This is rarely motivated by hostility.

In terms of sanitation, China can appear quite vulgar to westerners. Traditional Chinese medicine believes it is unhealthy to swallow phlegm, it is not uncommon to see Chinese people spitting in public. Also, it is not uncommon for small children to eliminate their bodily waste in public – in bushes, on the sidewalk, or even in train stations. Even adults do not cover their mouths when they cough or sneeze.

In general, China is not an overly polite country. In crowded situations, people are accustomed to pushing and shoving to get somewhere. For situations where people are meant to wait in line, the Chinese will usually try to jump ahead, or not form lines at all.

People will smoke everywhere, even in areas clearly labeled "no smoking allowed." However, Beijing now forbids smoking in restaurants.

Lastly, you may have heard of China's infamous censorship regime. You'll have a hard time accessing many US-based websites there, including Facebook, Twitter, and Gmail. If you absolutely need to use these sites, consider purchasing a VPN (Virtual Private Network) service for the duration of your trip.

Formalities

Saving Face
The Chinese tend to be very concerned about "saving face." So be considerate. Pointing out someone's mistake directly will cause him or her to "lose face." If necessary, try to take the person aside and tell them in private, and do it tastefully.

Pointing at Religious Statues
Pointing at statues of the Buddha and other deities with your index finger is considered very rude.

Drinking
When offered a drink in China, you are expected to take it. Otherwise, others at the table will keep pushing you. An excuse like "I don't feel like drinking" likely won't get you off the hook. Try to say, "I'm allergic to alcohol", or pretend that you are already drunk. Don't panic – foreigners are usually excused from much of these customs.

Costs

Mainland China is not as cheap as it used to be in the 1990s, but it is still quite affordable compared to western countries. If you are smart – find budget hotels or hostels, use public transit, and eat local food – you can live on a budget of around ¥200 to ¥300 a day as a traveler. However, Shanghai and Beijing are getting quite expensive, and entrance fees to tourist attractions and historical sites are increasing rapidly.

Tipping
In general, China is not a tipping country. Waiters, room service personnel, taxi drivers, and other service workers do not expect a tip, with the exception of hotels that cater to foreign clients.

Bargaining
You can still bargain over many things in China. A general rule of thumb is if a store is owned by a large company – international clothing brands, department stores, etc. – you should not try to bargain.

For almost everything else, it doesn't hurt to try! At malls with individual stalls or informal vendors, you can definitely bargain. Some restaurants, KTVs, and bars, will gladly send a free dish or two if you are spending a lot of money at the venue. In tourist shops and souvenir stalls, bargain!

For a beginner, it might be hard to know what price to offer to start negotiating. Depending on the good, anywhere from 5% to 50% is an appropriate starting point. In general, the more touristy a place is, the more discount you can ask for – 30% to 50% is common. For local places, 50% is too much. Try to walk around and compare to get a good sense of how much something is worth. If a proprietor is offering really low prices, it may be a sign the quality is not great.

Safety

Food and Water Sanitation
China has great food, so you should try everything. But be start – avoid small street food stalls unless it's in one of those famous food streets, or when you can tell it is very clean, and there is no danger of the food is undercooked. Poor hygiene can cause

bacterial or parasitic infection, especially in hot weather. Try to avoid seafood and raw meat unless you are in Beijing, Shanghai, or respectable venues in other large cities. Definitely abstain from these dishes on the street in summer. As a final precaution, bring diarrhea medication, and do not drink tap water in China.

Scams

Chinese can be friendly, but avoid any locals who appear overly friendly right away and invite you somewhere. What's known as the "teahouse scam" befalls foreigners often: in a tourist destination like Tian An Men Square, or a shopping district like Wang Fu Jing in Beijing, or Nanjing Road in Shanghai, a local comes up to you and strikes up a conversation in English. They show goodwill by helping you bargain and showing you around. After, they invite you to a café, teahouse, or a pub, where every item – a cup of tea, a biscuit, or a slice of fruit – is priced at an extortionate price. You will not be allowed to leave until you pay the astronomical tab. In some cases the scammer will convince you to pay at least half of the really big bill.

A similar scam is run by "art students" who invite you to art shops and force you to buy overpriced, worthless reproductions.

Pollution

Beijing is, according to some, the most polluted city in the world. Locals, expats, and visitors are all increasingly concerned with the air quality in the city. In addition, 16 of the most polluted cities in the world are in China. Be prepared for smog, especially if you have respiratory difficulties. Note that the quality of air varies depending on the weather. For example, very windy or rainy days will usually clear the sky of smog. Locals are in the habit of wearing facemasks on especially polluted days.

Outside Beijing and other heavily industrialized cities, China's air condition is not as bad. Cities in higher altitudes, like Provinces of

Yunnan, Sichuan, Xinjiang, Inner Mongolia, Tibet, and the outlying islands like Hainan, have pretty clear air.

Getting Around

Chinese traffic is notorious, especially in Shanghai, Beijing, and Hong Kong. Luckily, these cities have extensive subway systems. Use these whenever possible. They are the easiest way to get around – much cheaper than cabs, and there is no danger of getting stuck in endless traffic.

Crossing the Street and Traffic Rules
Be very careful when crossing the streets in China, even at green lights, because traffic rules are only followed haphazardly, and cars rarely yield to pedestrians. To be safe, follow locals when a large group is crossing. If you are on your own, look in every direction!

Due to cars occupying every lane of the road, bikes and motorcycles just do what they like and drive sometimes on the sidewalk. It's not a bad idea to walk in the road at night, as it is better lit than the sidewalk.

Chinese Taxis
Depending on the city, taxis charge a ¥5 to ¥14, with around ¥2 per kilometer charge. A trip in any given city should cost around ¥10 to ¥50. There is no luggage charge, but taxis in many cities hike the price at night. You are not expected to tip.

Some drivers will try to cheat tourists, especially foreigners, by taking a longer route, but this is not as common any more and should not be a problem. Usually, the price difference is minimal. But if you do feel seriously scammed, you can try to apply to the doorman at your hotel. It will likely only take a few sharp words for the driver to owe up to the deception.

Public Bathrooms

Outside major cities, going to a public bathroom can be unpleasant, or even repulsive. Carry your own packet of tissue paper since toilet paper is rarely provided, even if you had to pay to use the public bathroom – usually no more than one or two yuan.

More often than not, Chinese public bathrooms are equipped only with the squatting type of toilet, which may be a bit tricky for foreigners to use.

SURVIVAL CHINESE PHRASES

Mandarin Chinese is the official language of China. However, there are over 2,000 dialects in use in China, and in cities outside Beijing, you may hear the local dialect more than Mandarin.

Older Chinese most likely do not speak English, but more and more of the younger generation has been learning English in school for years. In smaller cities, fewer people will be able to speak Chinese.

To help getting around in China, try to learn a few basic phrases, and consider downloading a translator app like Google Translate, for when you are really in a bind trying to communicate with a loca.

In Hong Kong, the official language is Cantonese Chinese, but most people speak some Mandarin, and more people compared to the Mainland will speak a good amount of English.

Yes	shì
No	bú shì
Thank you	xìe xìe
Thank you very much	fei- cháng gàn xìe / henv gàn xìe
You're welcome	bu yong xie
Please	qíng
Excuse me	qivng ràng, dui bu qi
Hello	Ni hao
Goodbye	zài jiàn

So long	zài jiàn
Good morning	zao an-.
Good afternoon	wu an-.
Good evening	wan shàng hao.
Good night	wan an-.
I do not understand	wo bù míng bái / wo bù dong
How do you say this in [English]?	zhe yòng [yi-ng yu] zen me jiang?
Do you speak ...	ni hùi jiang ... ma?
English	yi-ng yu.
French	fá yu.
German	dé yu.
Spanish	xi- bán yá yu.
Chinese	pu to-ng hùa / hàn yu.
I	wo.
We	wov mén
You (singular, familiar)	ni.
You (singular, formal)	nín
You (plural)	ni mén
They	ta- mén
What is your name?	ni jiào shen me míng zi?
Nice to meet you.	hen gao- xìng yù jiàn ni.
How are you?	ni hao ma?
Good	hao.
Bad	bù hao.
So so	hái hao.
Wife	qi- zi.
Husband	zhàng fu-.
Daughter	nü er
Son	ér zi

Mother	ma- ma
Father	ba- ba
Friend	péng you.
Where is the bathroom? Where is the toilet?	xiv shou jian- zai- na li?
zero	líng
one	yi-.
two	èr
three	san-.
four	sì
five	wu.
six	lìu
seven	qi-.
eight	ba-.
nine	jiu.
ten	shí
eleven	shí yi-.
twelve	shí èr
thirteen	shí san-.
fourteen	shí sì
fifteen	shí wu.
sixteen	shí lìu
seventeen	shí qi-.
eighteen	shí ba.
nineteen	shí jiu.
twenty	èr shí
twenty one	èr shí yi-.
thirty	san- shí
forty	sì shí
fifty	wuv shí

sixty	liù shí
seventy	qi- shí
eighty	ba- shí
ninety	jiu shí
one hundred	yì bai.
one thousand	yì qian.
one million	yì bai wàn
How much does this cost?	zhe duo- shao qián?
What is this?	zhe shi shen me?
I'll buy it.	wov mai.
I would like to buy ...	wov yào mai ...
Do you have ...	ni you méi you ...
Do you accept credit cards?	ni jie- shòu xìn yòng ka ma?
Open	kai-.
Closed	guan-.
Postcard	míng xìn piàn
Stamps	yóu piào
A little	yi dian(r) er
A lot	hen duo-.
All	quán bù
Breakfast	zao can-.
Lunch	wu can-.
Dinner	wan can-.
Vegetarian	sù shí zhev.
Kosher	yóu tài hé fav shí wù
Cheers!	gan bei
Please bring the bill.	qingv jíe zhàng.
Bread	miàn bao-.
Beverage	yin liào
Coffee	ka- fei-.

Tea	chá
Juice	guo zhi-.
Water	shui.
Beer	pí jiu.
Wine	jiu.
Salt	yán
Pepper	hú jiao-.
Meat	roù
Beef	niú roù
Pork	zhu- roù
Fish	yú
Poultry	jia- qin.
Vegetable	cài
Fruit	shui guo.
Potato	ma líng shu.
Salad	sa- là
Dessert	tián pin.
Ice cream	bing- qi- lín / xue gào
Where is ...?	... zai na li?
How much is the fare?	che- fèi duo shao?
Ticket	piao
One ticket to ..., please.	yì zha-ng qù ... de piào.
Where are you going?	ni qù na li?
Where do you live?	ni zhù zài na li?
Train	huo che-.
Bus	gong- gòng qì che- / gong- che-.
Subway, Underground	dì tie.
Airport	fei- ji- chang.
Train station	huo che- zhàn

Bus station	gong- gòng qì che- zhàn / gong- che- zhàn
Subway station, Underground station	dì tie zhàn
Departure	chu- jìng
Arrival	rù jìng
Car rental agency	chu- zu- qì che chang.
Parking	tíng che- chang.
Hotel	lü' guan.
Room	kè fáng
Reservation	yù dìng
Are there any vacancies for tonight?	jin- wan you méi you kong- fáng?
No vacancies	kè man / méi you kong- fáng
Passport	hù zhào
Left	zuo.
Right	yòu
Straight	zhí
Up	shàng
Down	xià
Far	yuan.
Near	jìn
Long	cháng
Short	duan.
Map	dì tù
Tourist Information	liu yóu wèn xún chù
Post office	yóu jú
Museum	bó wú guan.
Bank	yín háng
Police station	jing chá jú
Hospital	yi- yuàn

Pharmacy, Chemists	yào fáng
Store, Shop	diàn
Restaurant	jiu lóu
School	xúe xiáo
Church	jiào táng
Restrooms	xi shou jian-.
Street	jie-.
Square	fang-, guang chang
Mountain	shan-.
Hill	shan- / qiu-.
Valley	shan- gu.
Ocean	haiv, yang
Lake	hú
River	hé
Swimming Pool	yóu yongv chí
Tower	ta.
Bridge	qiáo
What time is it?	jí dian zhòng le?
7:13, Seven thirteen	qi- dian shí san- fen-.
3:15, Three fifteen	san- dian shí wu fen-.
3:15, A quarter past three	san- dian yí kè
11:30, Eleven thirty	shí yi- dian san- shí fen-.
11:30, Half past eleven	shí yi- dian bàn
1:45, One forty-five	yi- dianv sì shí wu fen-.
1:45, A quarter till two	yi- dianv sì shí wu fen-.
Day	rì / tian-.
Week	xing- qi-.
Month	yùe.
Year	nián.
Monday	xing- qi- yi-.

Tuesday	xing- qi- èr
Wednesday	xing- qi- san-.
Thursday	xing- qi- sì
Friday	xing- qi- wu.
Saturday	xing- qi- liù
Sunday	xing- qi- rì / xing- qi- tiàn
January	yi- yùe
February	èr yùe
March	san- yùe
April	sì yùe
May	wu yùe
June	liù yùe
July	qì yùe
August	bà yùe
September	jiuv yùe
October	shí yùe
November	shí yi- yùe
December	shí èr yùe
Spring	chun-.
Summer	xià.
Fall, Autumn	qiu-.
Winter	dòng.
Today	jin- tian-.
Yesterday	zúo tian-.
Tomorrow	míng tian-.
Birthday	sheng- rì
Happy Birthday!	sheng- rì kuài lè!

CONCLUSION

We hope this pocket guide helps you navigate Shanghai and find the most memorable and authentic things to do, see, and eat.

Thank you for purchasing our pocket guide. After you've read this guide, we'd really appreciate your honest book review!

Sincerely,
The Wanderlust Pocket Guides Team

CREDITS

Cover design by Wanderlust Pocket Guide Design Team

COPYRIGHT AND DISCLAIMER

Best of Beijing

Made in the USA
San Bernardino, CA
29 November 2015